BERYL COOK

Private View

BERYL COOK
Private View

John Murray
Gallery Five

© Beryl Cook 1980

First published 1980
by John Murray (Publishers) Ltd
50 Albemarle Street, London W1X 4BD.
and Gallery Five Ltd, 14 Ogle Street, London W1P 7LG

Printed in Great Britain
by Caledonian Graphics Ltd

British Library Cataloguing in Publication Data
Cook, Beryl
    Private View.
    1. Cook, Beryl
    I. Title
    759.2   ND497.C/
    ISBN 0-7195-3728-2

Foreword

Few artists can have made such an immediate impact on the public as Beryl Cook. At one moment she was completely unknown; at the next, so it seemed, almost everyone had heard of her. First, a few paintings appeared quietly in the window of a remote country antique shop. Then there were exhibitions in Plymouth, in Bristol, in London; an article in a colour supplement, a television programme, a series of greetings cards and a highly successful book. Her rise was the more astonishing since she was completely untrained, and was already middle-aged by the time she began to paint.

Faced with such a series of events, the temptation is to discuss Beryl's art in the context of naïve art. This seems to me a mistake, for she is a highly sophisticated and original painter, whose work deserves to be taken on its own terms.

What are those terms? If one actually meets Beryl, one comes to understand them a little better. The pictures may seem extrovert, but she is not. For example, she is too shy to turn up at her own private views. Her pleasure is to stay in the background, observing.

And what an observer Beryl Cook is! It so happens that I was present when the ideas for two of the paintings in the present collection germinated. One is a portrait of my dog, a French bulldog called Bertie. Beryl came to see me for the first time, and he bounded up the stairs ahead of her, wearing his winter coat which is made from an old scarf. A few days later his picture arrived in the post. The picture called *Leather Bar* had its beginnings the same evening. I took Beryl and her husband John to a pub. There was a fight, and we saw someone being thrown out by the bouncers.

The point about these two incidents is that they both happened in a flash. No-one was carrying a camera; there was no opportunity to make sketches. But somehow the essentials of the scene registered themselves indelibly with

Beryl, and she was able to record them later in an absolutely convincing and authoritative way.

The fact is she has two very rare gifts, not one. She has a magnificent visual memory, and at the same time she is able to compress, re-arrange and simplify what she sees until it makes a completely convincing composition. Bertie's portrait, with its plump backside and bow legs, is more like Bertie than his reflection in a mirror – it catches the absolute essentials of his physique and personality.

But these gifts are just the foundation of what Beryl Cook does. She has a very keen feeling for pictorial rhythm. The picture of *Dustmen*, for instance, has a whirling rhythm which is emphasised by the movement of their large hands in red rubber gloves – these big hands are often a special feature of Beryl's pictures. The English artist she most closely resembles in this respect is Stanley Spencer.

Details such as the ones I have been describing are, of course, just the kind of thing to appeal to a professional art critic. Important as they are, they would not in themselves account for the impact she has had on the public.

Basically, I think this impact is due to two things. When Beryl paints an actual, everyday scene – and I confess these are the pictures I prefer – the smallest detail is immediately recognisable. Her people, for example, seem to fit into a kind of Beryl Cook stereotype, with their big heads and rolypoly bodies. Yet they are in fact brilliantly accurate portraits. Walking round Plymouth with her, I am always recognising people who have made an appearance in her work. Indeed, her vision is so powerful that one tends ever after to see the individual in the terms Beryl has chosen for him.

The other reason for her success is almost too obvious to be worth mentioning – it is her marvellous and distinctly salty sense of humour. *My Fur Coat* is a kind of transcription of a seaside postcard. The incident is amusing in a rumbustious way, but what makes the picture really memorable is the expression on the face of the bowler-hatted gentleman who is being offered this unexpected treat. The humour operates even in pictures which aren't obviously 'funny'. There is something very endearing, for instance, in the two road sweepers with Plymouth lighthouse looming behind them.

A sense of humour may be a good reason for success with the public. It is, alas, also one which tends to devalue Beryl's work with professional art buffs. Her work contains too much life to be real art as they understand it.

This seems to me nonsense, and dangerous nonsense at that. Beryl does what artists have traditionally done – she comments on the world as she perceives it. And the same time she re-arranges what she sees to make a pattern of shapes and colours on a flat surface – a pattern which is more than the sum of its individual parts because it has the mysterious power to enhance and vivify our own responses to the visible.

I suspect Beryl's paintings will be remembered and cherished long after most late 20th-century art is forgotten. What they bring us is a real sense of how ordinary life is lived in our own time, a judgement which is the more authoritative for the humour and lightness of touch.

Edward Lucie-Smith

The Art Class

This is one side of a signboard for the Plymouth Arts Centre, and stems from the stories my mother used to tell us of her experiences of evening art classes she joined at a rather advanced age. They made her laugh so much I doubt whether she can have learned a great deal, but she enjoyed the few she attended. And this is how I feel some of the results might have been greeted.

Musicians

The other side of the signboard and what I imagine to
be a serious trio enjoying some chamber music. I felt
I really must get the instruments right in this case
and borrowed a book from the library to assist me. It
did take me some considerable time writing the music
for them and I hope it is in keeping with the exquisite
pleasure they are feeling.

Strawberry Pickers

We took our granddaughter Alexa out to the strawberry fields last summer. She ate strawberries, John picked them, and I just stood about, unlike these people here. The plants were all painted from one I have in a pot at home, turning it round to get different views of the leaves. I then found it extremely difficult to get the colours of the clothes right and grew most savage with the painting, finally banishing it altogether until I could forgive its faults. As I paint on wood I'm unable to attack them with knives when they won't behave so I send them to Coventry.

Red Hot Poker

Look – no humans! Just Teddy the tortoise and
Lottie peering through the undergrowth. I watched
him desperately tugging away at a leaf one day, as did
Lottie, who follows his movements (when he *is*
moving) with the greatest interest. He didn't succeed
in shifting the Red Hot Poker, or even in removing a
leaf, so he staggered off to trample down the more
convenient tomato plants.

My Fur Coat

Having decided to paint my fur coat displayed to its
best advantage – from the back and open wide – it
only needed a gentleman passer-by to complete the
picture. Believe me, it was not easy getting *just* the
right expression of mingled horror and pleasure on
his face. Now which one of you would like to buy a
very distinctive fur coat, for standing about on street
corners in the twilight?

Park-keepers

I would like to be able to paint the spectacular skies I
see sometimes on cold winter mornings, but I'm
afraid my efforts turn out to be rather feeble.
However, here is my version of the Hoe in winter,
with two park-keepers. They and the gardeners are
very good here and are just starting work when we see
them early in the morning when taking Bonzo for a
walk. During the summer there are lovely displays of
flowers in the beds on the Hoe and through the City,
with no restrictions about walking on the grass either,
which is very nice.

Applause

Who mentioned bananas? I'm
afraid I gave way completely to a
fondness for large, fat fingers in this
painting – originally intended as a
picture of James Galway.
Gradually the hands got larger and
James Galway smaller, and here he
is receiving rapturous applause at a
lovely concert he gave us last year
in Plymouth.

The Market

This is one of several pictures I have painted of our Market, visited by me most mornings. Early too, as I like to see all the fruit and vegetables being arranged as well as being on the spot when the best bargains are to be had from the junk stalls. The girl in the front, expertly manoeuvring both baby and shopping trolly, wasn't quite in the market when I saw her but heading rapidly towards it.

Sailors & Seagulls

I often watch the seagulls but they
are not very obliging about staying
still for me to draw them and I
eventually had to use some I found
in a book for this painting. The
sailors are eyeing a likely prospect
just about to enter the picture,
whilst Bonzo waits hopefully for
someone to throw his ball. He's
actually there because he was just
the right shape to fit the pathway.

Tesco

Once a week we go shopping for our groceries, and the necessities – such as beer. I like supermarkets, with all the activity and bustle. Although there have been many attempts this is the first time I have succeeded in getting a picture, and possibly the last too I decided after painting all those tins. The assistant with the large foot is not flying through the air, but climbing up to stack the top shelf.

Three Ladies

Now aren't these lovely. They arrived in the Phoenix
one hot summer's night, with a sort of entourage of
gentlemen, and paused for a while at a table near us
which gave me a chance to admire their finery. In the
painting I've given one of them a very pretty necklace
I bought in the market.

Bingo

I'm sorry to say this is not me winning the big prize,
but someone sitting very close to us. I'm not sure if I
shall be able to shout when I *do* win, I'm too
frightened of finding out I've crossed off all the
wrong numbers. It was fairly easy to draw this
picture but I haven't yet managed to do one of the
outside of the Bingo hall, which I also like very much.

Bumper Cars

I don't like fairs, but do like the people they attract. I saw the two French sailors walking with their girlfriends and soon afterwards squeezed them into one of these bumper cars, which were much admired by me for their spotless and highly coloured condition. This is one of the very few paintings I have liked as soon as I had finished it, possibly because I found it easy to both draw and paint.

The Lovers

This is a corner of our garden, my view in fact each
time I slump onto the sunbathing mat, and a
favourite spot of Cedric's. After two unsuccessful
attempts to get him placed in the centre of the foliage
I gave it up and put in some lovers instead. One of
them turned out to be George, who had just had his
hair permed, and I liked it so much I gave them both
the curls.

Brian on a Motorbike

Brian and I would really like to have a customised
motor bike. He will drive it very carefully at 30
m.p.h. and I will sit in the sidecar, both dressed from
head to toe in all the right gear. We have discussed
this many times, our clothes growing ever more
elaborate and the bike more fantastic. However, this
small painting I did for Brian is probably the nearest
we shall get to it.

Tennis

I was very tired indeed after arranging this strenuous
game of tennis for a friend of ours, Tony. As soon as
the picture was framed I realised I needed to find his
opponent some real hair, and used an old hairpiece of
Teresa's, which fitted perfectly. So far I have not
succeeded in keeping the hair curled and may have to
perm it. Or shall I just go back to painting?

Dustbinmen

I little knew that this picture I painted of the dustbinmen cheerfully getting rid of our rubbish would be all that I'd see of them for a month or so, since the very next day they all went out on strike. I had gone out to open the back gate for them and liked all the bustle and activity going on, especially with the large rubber gloves. Not *quite* so large or tomato red in reality, I suspect.

Two Greek Gods

I had been gazing in wonder at a small cutting from the *Sunday Times*, showing a line-up of muscle men for a Mr Universe contest, and suddenly decided to give all their bodies to friends. As I had to use a magnifying glass (it was a *very* small cutting) I soon realised I might be ten years working on this masterpiece and settled for the only two I had managed to draw – Lionel and Eric.

Joe's Shoes

Here is Joe wearing one of his favourite outfits. I was
not fortunate enough to see the shoes for he liked
them so much he wore them out, but I liked the
sound of them so much I decided to paint them
anyway. I'm always interested in the fashions as they
come and go, particularly the shoes, and am very
indignant when I can't persuade my daughter-in-law
Teresa to wear the bargains I purchase from junk shops.

Restaurant Chartier

We spent a few days in Paris last year and this is the students' restaurant we queued up to get into almost every night. How I loved it all, the atmosphere, marble tables, brass fittings, even the noise. I discovered, as usual, that none of this is easy to paint and in the end concentrated on the waiters' uniforms and the quantity of plates carried on their arms. I'm particularly proud of the bald head in the front.

'Ullo Chéri

From the restaurant we'd slowly weave our way
(from café table to café table) up to Place Pigalle to
join the sightseers, and generally ended the evening
opposite these two. The fetching get-up of the one in
shorts appealed not only to me but many others
judging from the number of times she disappeared
and re-appeared on her corner.

Little Chef

It seems I spend rather a lot of time with food – buying, eating and painting it – and here is an old favourite. I became aware of the small hunched figure in the dark corner when I was waiting for my waffle with ice cream, cream and chocolate sauce to arrive, and realised she'd had a *very* hard day. I like to think I so often paint food because of the colours, but could it be greed?

Two Men and Small Lady

I painted this some years ago when, apparently, patchwork trousers were in vogue. I remember how taken I was with this very little lady, wearing a large fur coat and deep in conversation with her friends. I admire Stanley Spencer's paintings very much and decided to try and paint it to look exactly like one of his, and so I also remember my intense disappointment when it turned out to be one of mine instead.

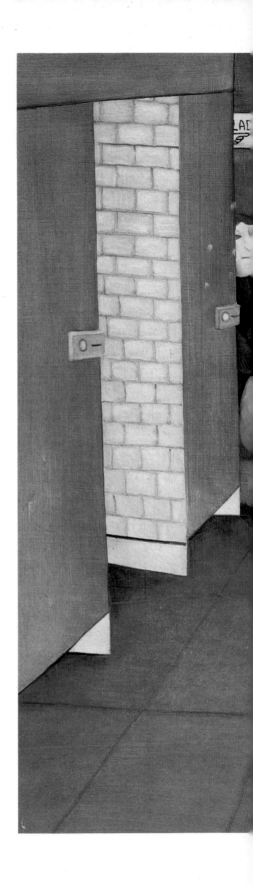

Ladies

This scene greeted me when I found a
shabby old 'ladies' at Victoria Station,
and I dutifully joined the patient queue.
It did rather surprise me that we all so
uncomplainingly shuffled along, jumping
to obey the shouted commands. One poor
soul mistakenly held a door open for the
next eager occupant, and had to be Very
Sternly Reprimanded.
She won't do that again.

Leather Bar

I am the one in the front leaning forward, pushing him out of the door! That is not strictly true, but he *is* wearing my jacket purchased the day after we had visited this bar in London, and I hope I'm not similarly affected after a drink in a punk bar we are going to soon. I noticed that as first one body, and then another, were rushed through the doors everyone swayed towards them, me included, and I have tried to show this.

Oh how difficult it is painting spilled beer! For some time I sat in front of the picture and painted nothing, then I tried throwing paint on to make a splash. After that fiasco I poured cold tea onto a red tray, broke a milk bottle beside it, had a drink of beer and painted what I saw. I hope you can see it too.

B. Cook

Bang's Disco

I felt I had taken a step forward with this picture, in managing to paint most of it in one colour – blue. It was a year or so ago that we went to this Disco, when everyone dressed in jeans. I found it very exciting, with little outbursts of dancing round the tables as well as on the floor and I was so eager to try and paint this I drew it as soon as we got back home again from London.

Mum in Hammock

This is Sunday afternoon in a garden in Reading many, many years ago. The pretty one in the sailor suit is ME and the others my sisters, Cynthia, Mary and Freda. Mary is eating her greatest treat – a large meringue – whilst the rest of us busily tease and provoke each other. We rarely spent more than a quarter of an hour together without an argument or fight and my mother, long accustomed to the sound of thuds, blows and shrill threats, takes a rest in the hammock. Just out of sight, in the garden next door, John would be aiming stones – and very accurate he was too.

Attending the Plants

And here we are, John and I, a hundred or so years
later. John has progressed from stones to something I
won't tell you about, except to say he gets it off
Dartmoor where the wild ponies are, and is busy
preparing it for his tomatoes. This was painted on a
piece of wardrobe our son had been dismantling in
the garage, where this scene is taking place. The fact
that we are hopeless gardeners does not deter us in
the least: every year we plan, plant and pot up a new
batch of failures.

Acknowledgements

The following have kindly given permission for their paintings to be reproduced:

The Art Class and *Musicians*, Plymouth Arts Centre; *Strawberry Pickers*, John Cleverdon; *Red Hot Poker*, Martin Bluff; *My Fur Coat* and *Bangs*, David Walser; *Sailors and Seagulls*, Jim Fardon; *Three Ladies*, Private Collection; *Bumper Cars*, Richard Dent; *The Lovers*, Mr. & Mrs. Tahany; *Brian on a Motorbike*, Brian Pearce; *Tennis* and *Attending the Plants*, Tony Martin; *Two Greek Gods*, Portal Gallery Ltd; *Joe's Shoes* and *Self-portrait (writing)*, Joe Whitlock Blundell; *Little Chef*, Freda Purssell; *Two Men and Small Lady*, Alec Forbes; *Leather Bar*, *Self-portrait (in leather)* and *Bertie*, Edward Lucie-Smith; *Applause*, Alexander Gallery Ltd.

Photography: Rodney Todd-White & Son Ltd
Design: Ian Craig

Beryl Cook's paintings are sold in London through Portal Gallery Ltd

A limited edition print of *The Art Class* is available from Alexander Gallery Ltd, Bristol

Greetings cards of a number of Beryl Cook's paintings are available from Gallery Five Ltd, London